W9-BVN-277

DATE DUE
09/15/00

# RISKY BUSINESS

# Photojournalist

## *In the Middle of Disaster*

*By*

KEITH ELLIOT GREENBERG

*Photographs by John Isaac*

A BLACKBIRCH PRESS BOOK

WOODBRIDGE, CONNECTICUT

Published by Blackbirch Press, Inc.
260 Amity Road
Woodbridge, CT 06525

Printed in the United States of America

10 9 8 7 6 5 4 3 2 1

**Photo Credits**
**Cover:** Courtesy U.N. Photo Archives
**Page 13:** © Bruce Glassman
**All other photos:** Courtesy UNICEF and United Nations/John
Isaac

**Library of Congress Cataloging-in-Publication Data**

Greenberg, Keith Elliot.
    Photojournalist/by Keith Elliot Greenberg—1st ed.
        p.    cm. — (Risky business)
    Includes bibliographical references and index.
    Summary: Describes the experiences of a United Nations
photographer who has recorded the terrors of war in such places
as Lebanon, Cambodia, and Bosnia.
    ISBN 1-56711-157-2 (alk. paper)
    1. Isaac, John. 2. War photographers—United States—
Biography—Juvenile literature. [1. Isaac, John.  2. War photographers.  3. Photographers. ] I. Title. II. Series: Risky business.
TR140.I75G74   1996
770'.92—dc20
[B]                                                        95-22683
                                                               CIP
                                                                AC

Things seemed quiet enough, as John Isaac rode in the caravan through the bullet-scarred streets of Bosnia. Just a few years before, the area had been peaceful and beautiful. Snow-capped mountains provided a comforting background for Bosnia's capital city, Sarajevo. In 1984, the Winter Olympics had even been held there. But now, things were very different. Now, the Bosnians and Serbs were at war. Now there were cannons in the hills, aimed at Sarajevo's people.

As an official photographer
for the United Nations,
John Isaac travels the world.

Despite the great danger, John Isaac came to Sarajevo to do his job. He didn't care about the politics and the hatred between the Bosnians and the Serbs. As one of the official photographers for the United Nations (U. N.) he was in Bosnia to document the events of this place. The U.N. had been trying to get the different sides in the war to agree to a truce. While the war continued, the United Nations International Children's Emergency Fund—or UNICEF—offered aid to young people who were cut off from the rest of the world by the fighting.

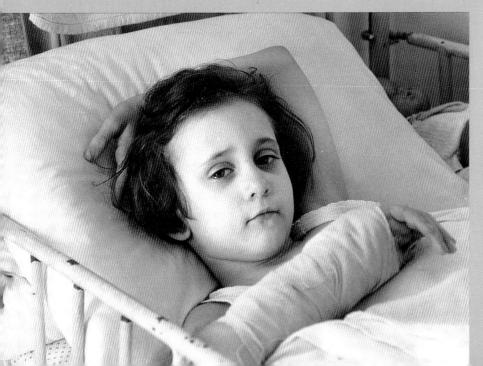

A young Bosnian girl with an arm wound stares out from her hospital bed in Sarajevo.

UNICEF workers deliver sleeping bags to a needy home in Sarajevo. Inset: Bosnian children show off the jogging suits they received from UNICEF workers who were distributing supplies.

John's assignment was to take pictures of the UNICEF workers bringing food, clothing, and medicine into the troubled area. John expected difficulties—when war is raging, nothing is ever easy.

When the jeep stopped at a checkpoint manned by Serbian fighters, John did what came naturally. He stepped out of the vehicle and began taking photographs. Suddenly, one of the fighters came up behind him with a large knife.

John couldn't speak Serbo-Croatian—the language of the region—but he knew that the man with the knife didn't like him. The soldier believed John was a spy for the rival Bosnians. A French UNICEF worker pulled John back into the jeep, but the fighter yanked him out and threw him against an armored vehicle. By now, two other men had joined in. They were holding guns on John.

"I was scared out of my mind," John recalls. "I thought I was going to die."

8

Luckily, several brave UNICEF workers stepped between John and his accusers. They convinced the fighters that John worked for the United Nations—an organization devoted to peace, not war. After much argument, John was allowed to leave.

During his 14 years of covering all kinds of U. N. missions, John never thought he'd be personally attacked. In fact, he had gotten used to being in countries that were torn apart by war. Sometimes, he took extra precautions, such as putting on a bullet-proof vest and helmet. But, most of the time, he took the same chances as the people caught in the middle of the conflict.

**Destroyed buildings line the streets of the Croatian city of Vukovar.**
**Inset: John takes many chances as he tries to photograph the effects of war.**

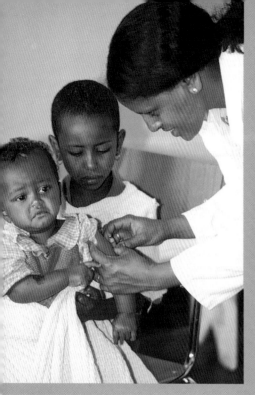

"This might sound funny, but day to day, it's not so bad," says John. "You're with the U. N. and you see them helping people, so that makes you feel good. Of course, it's dangerous. But people say that living in big cities is dangerous, too.

"You get encouraged by the people you meet. Their houses blow up, and they leave the city for a couple of days, then come back and rebuild. As much as possible, they try to live a normal life. It's only when you see guns pointed at you that you realize how dangerous it really is."

**Top: A UNICEF medical worker gives a shot to a young girl in Ethiopia.**
**Bottom: A man and boy support each other as they learn to walk with artificial limbs in Afghanistan.**

John photographs the children of a village in Nepal.

Examples of John's work from around the world include (top) children celebrating Namibian independence; (bottom left) a Nepali girl; and (bottom right) a sunset on a beach in India.

John—who lives close to U. N. world headquarters in New York City—didn't grow up dreaming of taking pictures of war scenes. He was raised in the city of Madras, in India, and moved to New York in 1968. After applying for a number of jobs, he became a U. N. messenger. Meanwhile, he spent his spare time taking pictures—a hobby he had loved since childhood. When the U. N. had a photography contest for employees, he entered a photo he had taken in India. John not only won first prize, but also a job in the U.N.'s photography department.

For several years, he worked at U. N. headquarters. There, he took pictures of the General Assembly—the place where United Nations representatives from around the world debate issues and vote on proposals.

**United Nations headquarters in New York.**

In 1968, John was invited to accompany a U. N. mission to Lebanon in the Middle East. Israel had invaded the country and now U.N. forces were trying to supervise a peaceful withdrawal. Because U.N. soldiers were trying to calm the situation, they were known as "peacekeepers."

John knew very little about the circumstances in Lebanon. "I didn't even realize I was going to a war," he says. "I was just happy to be flying to another country on a big assignment."

U.N. soldiers stand guard at an observation post in South Lebanon.

John has recorded many dramatic scenes with his camera over the years.

One of his first tasks was traveling with U. N. diplomats who were paying a visit to Yasser Arafat, head of the Palestinian Liberation Organization, or PLO. Arafat had many enemies, and he didn't want people to know the location of his hideout in Lebanon's capital of Beirut. John was blindfolded, so he wouldn't know where he was being taken. When he arrived, he immediately put his camera to his eye and started snapping.

"It was my first big assignment, and I was really excited," he explains. "We were on a block of all apartment buildings. There were about 150 windows on the block, and every one of them was stacked with sandbags, with machine guns pointing out. Nobody wanted me to show where Arafat was staying."

On the same trip, John had his first brush with death as a photojournalist. As he drove down a street, a large rocket-propelled grenade shot in front of him. It blew a hole in a wall and blasted through a building.

18

Inset: John travels on an elephant in India.
Below: On assignment in Iraq, John stops to speak with some soldiers.

"I'm not embarrassed to tell you that it was scary," John admits. "Every time something like this happens, it scares me. But I've always felt like I had a shield around me. Other war photographers have told me the same thing. It's like a guardian angel watching out for you."

The next year, John found himself in Southeast Asia, in Cambodia. Vietnam had invaded the country, and over 40,000 people were fleeing. John took a touching photograph of an elderly woman who'd left everything behind as she escaped to Thailand. The U. N. released the picture and several major magazines printed it.

**John photographs the daily life of a village in Cambodia.**

John's moving portrait of an elderly Cambodian refugee and child.

One day, John received a telephone call from a woman in California. She'd seen the photo of the old lady, and recognized her. It was her grandmother, but they'd lost touch five years before. With John's help, the family was united again.

"That was one of my happiest moments," he says. "I felt that, by being there and taking that picture, I helped an entire family."

**John takes a moment to relax with a family in Jordan.**

ot all of John's work is filled with suffering and destruction. Through the years, he has also had many pleasant experiences as a photo-journalist. He's watched the United Nations build schools, vaccinate children, and help bring people back to their homelands after war. But the bitterness, bloodshed, and misery he has witnessed have also left some emotional scars.

**Above: A Chinese man enjoys some melon. Below: John shows his equipment to children in Mali.**

During the Persian Gulf War of 1990–1991, the United States led a U. N. force against Iraq. The goal was to force Iraq to leave Kuwait, a tiny country it had invaded. As Iraq retreated, its soldiers burned many of Kuwait's oil wells. Wanting to get the best pictures, John positioned himself close to the fires. As he took his shots, black smoke filled his lungs. For more than a year afterwards, he was coughing up black particles. For a war photographer, however, these dangers are worthwhile if the photographs are good.

Soldiers watch the rising flames of a burning oil well in Kuwait.

25

**Disabled and displaced children stand outside a UNICEF aid facility in Afghanistan.**

Many of the dangers and events John sees are not easy for him to forget. During his trip to Bosnia, he became dizzy as he photographed a young boy who had been burned all over his body. Watching the youngster's suffering, John started to cry.

"Why are you crying?" the boy asked.

"I'm crying because I can see you feel so bad," John said.

"Don't worry," the boy said. "I'll be alright."

Happily, the youngster's prediction came true. The U.N. sent him and other injured children to France, where doctors operated and the boy recovered.

A son comforts his mother, who was injured when a grenade landed in her Sarajevo basement.

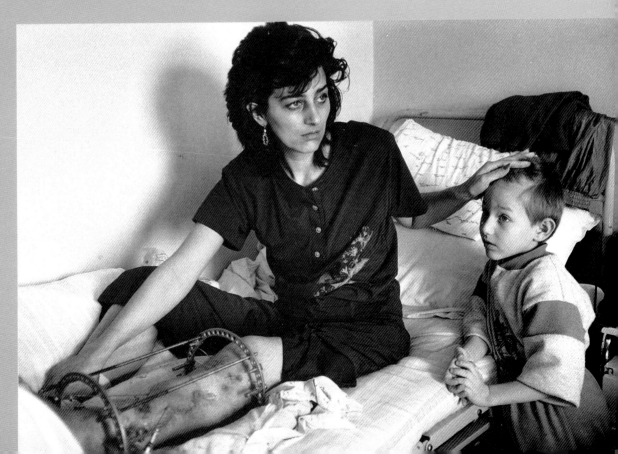

In 1994, John had what he considers the toughest assignment of his life. He was sent to the African country of Rwanda, where members of the Hutu and Tutsi tribes were slaughtering each other. There was death and suffering every-where. Bodies lay in the streets, without anyone to take them away.

"It was terrible," John recalls. "The people would be buried and nobody would remember them. I was so upset, I could hardly take any pictures."

UNICEF had set up a camp in Rwanda for "unaccompanied children"—youngsters who were either lost or orphaned. As soon as John entered to

take photographs, a bright-eyed boy said to him, "You look like my father, will you adopt me?"

John didn't answer. But, as he drove away from the camp, he was nearly in tears.

Above: Refugee children at a U.N. camp scramble for scraps of food.
Below: A Rwandan baby at a refugee camp.

After Rwanda, John returned to New York. But he couldn't stop thinking about the boy he had met. At night, John's wife, Jeannette, would wake him and say, "You were screaming in your sleep." During work at U. N. headquarters, John would

John looks through the large collection of photos at his U.N. office.

suddenly start crying for no reason. Finally, he went to a therapist to help him deal with the stress of being a war photographer.

"When you're home, safe in your bed, you think about all those people you wanted to help but couldn't," John says.

Still, he's looking forward to traveling with the United Nations on assignment again. "It's important," he says. "My photographs are a record of history—and proof of just how terrible war is."

In between assignments, John works at the United Nations in New York City.

# FURTHER READING

Bratman, Fred. *War in the Persian Gulf.* Brookfield, CT: Millbrook, 1991.

Evans, Art. *First Photos: How Kids Can Take Great Pictures.* Redondo Beach, CA: Photo Data Research, 1993.

Greene, Carol. *The United Nations.* Chicago, IL: Childrens, 1983.

Ricciuti, Edward. *War in Yugoslavia: The Breakup of a Nation.* Brookfield, CT: Millbrook, 1993.

Ross, Stewart. *United Nations.* Chicago, IL: Watts, 1990.

# INDEX